Make the World New
The Poetry of Lillian Allen

Make the World New
The Poetry of Lillian Allen

Selected
with an
introduction by
Ronald Cummings
and an
afterword by
Lillian Allen

lps
LAURIER POETRY SERIES

WLU PRESS
WILFRID LAURIER
UNIVERSITY PRESS

Wilfrid Laurier University Press acknowledges the support of the Canada Council for the Arts for our publishing program. We acknowledge the financial support of the Government of Canada through the Canada Book Fund for our publishing activities. Funding provided by the Government of Ontario and the Ontario Arts Council. This work was supported by the Research Support Fund.

Library and Archives Canada Cataloguing in Publication

Title: Make the world new : the poetry of Lillian Allen / selected with an introduction by Ronald Cummings and an afterword by Lillian Allen.
Other titles: Poems. Selections
Names: Allen, Lillian, 1951– author, writer of afterword. | Cummings, Ronald, editor.
Series: Laurier poetry series.
Description: Series statement: Laurier poetry series | Includes bibliographical references.
Identifiers: Canadiana (print) 20210223146 | Canadiana (ebook) 20210223243 | ISBN 9781771124959 (softcover) | ISBN 9781771124966 (EPUB) | ISBN 9781771124973 (PDF)
Classification: LCC PS8551.L5554 A6 2021 | DDC C811/.54—dc23

Front cover image: *The wheel of abundance* by Ehiko Odeh.
Cover design by Gary Blakeley.
Interior design by Mike Bechthold.

This book is printed on FSC® certified paper. It contains recycled materials and other controlled sources, is processed chlorine free, and is manufactured using biogas energy.

Printed in Canada

Table of Contents

Foreword

I am happy to serve as the general editor for the Laurier Poetry Series, the development and growth of which I have followed from its early days. My gratitude goes to Neil Besner and Brian Henderson, who conceived of the Laurier Poetry Series in 2002 as a way to offer a more robust selection of a single poet's work than could be found in an anthology. In 2004, the Laurier Poetry Series launched the first volume, Catherine Hunter's selection of the poems of Lorna Crozier, *Before the First Word*. Neil served as General Editor for all volumes until he was joined in 2016 by Brian, when he left his role as WLU Press's Director. In an act of commitment to poetry publication that is nothing short of inspiring, the Laurier Poetry Series expanded to a list of thirty-three fascinating titles under their leadership.

The retirement of the original editors has given me a surprising historical jolt. But thinking historically is a good way to revisit the original plans for the series, and to think towards the future. Under my editorial eye, the series will retain its original aim to produce volumes of poetry made widely available to new readers, including undergraduate students at universities or colleges, and to a general readership who wish for "more poetry in their poetry." WLU Press also retains its commitment to produce beautiful volumes and to alert readers to poems that remain vital to thinking about urgencies of the contemporary moment. It is a reality that poetry books are produced in smaller print runs and often on a shoestring, and as a consequence, original collections of poetry tend to go out of print too quickly and far too precipitously. The series has the added goal of bringing poems from out-of-print collections back into the public eye and the public discourse. The Press's commitment to the work of literary studies includes choosing editors for each volume who can reflect deeply on the body of work, as well as inviting original afterwords from the poets themselves.

As we embark of this next turn of the series, access is our watchword. Canadian literature has undeniably had a checkered history of exclusionary practices, so who gets the nod and who takes part in discussions—as readers and as writers—of Canadian poetry? In the classroom, it is my privilege and my task to introduce a generation of students to the practice of reading poetry as a vital thread in cultural, social, and political conversations, conversations that challenge ideas about Canada and seek to illuminate and bring to consciousness better futures. For that work, I want access to as many voices on the page, and as robust a selection of poems from those voices, as I can get my hands on. This is the language of the bibliophile, the craver of books, the person whose pedagogical pleasure comes from putting poetry books into the hands of others and saying, simply, "Read this, and we'll talk." Multi-author anthologies do not always usefully demonstrate to readers how a poet's work shifts and changes over the years, nor do they always display the ways that a single poet's poems speak to and with and sometimes usefully against one another. I want at my elbow, in every discussion, inside and outside the classroom, our best poetic practitioners. I want books that offer not just a few poems, but dozens: selected volumes not only by the splashiest prize winners but also significantly by poets who have been carrying a full cultural backpack for decades. I also want to showcase new and prolific voices who have taken off like rockets. For this, I am grateful for the chance to bring these poets to you, or bring them back to you. Turn is sometimes a return and sometimes a revolution. Neil and Brian started this series off with a bang, and now it's time to light another fuse.

The volume you hold in your hands sizzles. Read this, and we'll talk.

—*Tanis MacDonald*
General Editor

Biographical Note

Lillian Allen was born in Jamaica. She grew up in a prominent family in Spanish Town, with an extended family network living in close proximity. The boundaries between family and community were not always fixed and Allen has often linked her investment in an ethic of community activism and care and her commitment to working class solidarity with these early formative experiences.

School and church were central pillars of community life. Allen attended St. Jago High School, one of the oldest continuously running schools in the Western hemisphere. She has noted that within her family, her generation was the first among a small number of people in the community to complete primary school and high school education. She attended the Methodist and Baptist churches and her father was a leader in the community and in the church. Some of her earliest experiences of performing poetry publicly were at church, school, and community events. She has also linked her early love of art to the creativity of her mother who made everything look beautiful and magical and who was a seamstress who also practiced embroidery while doing the daily work of caring for and raising a family of ten siblings.

Allen moved to Kitchener in 1969 to join her sister who had by then migrated to Canada for work. She moved to New York City in 1970 to study at CUNY where she took courses in Communications and Black Studies. During her time in NYC, she also worked at the publication *Caribbean Daily* where an early version of her well-known poem "I Fight Back" was first published.

In 1973, Allen returned to Jamaica to join what she called the "socialist revolution" that was taking place as the country turned towards democratic socialism. She worked with the Ministry of Education writing curriculum material and started a magazine called *MinEd*.

Allen moved to Toronto after about a year in Jamaica. She subsequently completed a BA in English and Creative Writing at York University. She also worked as the executive director of Black Education Project in the late 70s and then as a community legal worker in Regent Park and as an education coordinator for Immi-Can youth project. In the early 90s, she developed and initiated programs for youth such as Fresh Elements and Fresh Arts.

Allen has published several print volumes and sound recordings of her poetry. In 1982 she published the chapbook *Rhythm an' Hardtimes*. This was followed by *The Teeth of the Whirlwind* (1984) and by three books of verse for children: *If You See Truth* (1987), *Why Me* (1991) and *Nothing But a Hero* (1992). These independent publishing efforts led to the establishment of Well Versed, a publishing company formed in collaboration with Maureen Fitzgerald who worked at Women's Press. During the 1990s, Allen published *Women Do This Every Day* (1993) with Women's Press and *Psychic Unrest* (1999) with Insomniac Press.

Allen's albums *Revolutionary Tea Party* and *Conditions Critical* won Juno Awards in 1987 and 1989 respectively. Her other poetry recordings include *Dub Poetry: The Poetry of Lillian Allen* (1983), *De dub poets* (with Clifton Joseph and Devon Haughton, 1985), *Curfew Inna B.C.* (1985), *Let the Heart See* (1987), *Nothing But a Hero* (1992), *Freedom & Dance* (1999) and *Anxiety* (2012). Her work has been featured in Canadian and international media. In 1989, Allen's poem "Unnatural Causes" was the subject of a NFB short film. In 1993, she co-produced and co-directed the documentary *Blak Wi Blakk*, about the life and work of the dub poet Mutabaruka. Between 2003 and 2005, she hosted *Wordbeat*, a CBC radio series on poetry and spoken word and in 2006, her work was the subject of an episode of the television series *Heart of a Poet*.

Named a foremother of Canadian poetry by the League of Canadian Poets in 1992, Allen is the recipient of numerous other awards and fellowships including the Margo Bindhardt Award, the City of Toronto Cultural Champion Award, and the William P. Hubbard Award for Race Relations. She is an Executive Member of the Canadian Commission for UNESCO, and was a major influence in establishing the highly-acclaimed International Spoken Word Program at the Banff Centre for Fine Arts in Alberta. In 2000–2001, she was the Distinguished Writer-in-Residence at the University of Windsor and later became the first Canada Council Writer-in-Residence at Queen's University. She received an Honorary

Doctorate from Wilfrid Laurier University in 2016. Allen is a professor at OCAD University in Toronto where she spearheaded the development and establishment of the university's Bachelors of Fine Arts program in creative writing.

See Lillian Allen's website at: https://lillianallen.ca/

Introduction
Making Wor(l)ds Anew: Lillian Allen's Poetics

The first time I heard Lillian Allen's poetry I was sitting in a university lecture hall in Kingston, Jamaica. Her clear voice, against that dub rhythm, insisted a radical urgency into that hot October morning and wailed against colonial and contemporary oppressions calling for freedom, justice, and dignity as necessary social rights/rites. I have been thinking a lot about my own introduction to Lillian's work as I sit to write the introduction to this book. I have also been asking friends about their first encounters with Lillian Allen's poetry. One tells me, "In the very early 1990s, I bought *Revolutionary Tea Party* on cassette tape. I used to play it at family gatherings and people would sing along."[1] Another friend tells me about how copies of *Women Do This Every Day* were passed between community organizers and activists making language to resist racist and gendered forms of oppression.[2] Another story is told of the book being given to new arrivants from the Caribbean to Canada as a kind of reference guide on how to survive Canadian racism and as something to keep close to help you live a little better up in this cold place.[3] Still another friend tells me how "Lillian's work has influenced two solid generations of spoken word and performance poets ... That achievement, of creating a multi-generational community of the word, and of helping to speak a kind of hybridized Caribbean/Canadian poetic consciousness into being, is really remarkable. It articulates us all."[4] These responses and narratives speak to the vital and continued influence and impact of Lillian Allen's poetry and why her work remains important today.

I begin with these various accounts of poetic encounters for a number of reasons. First, they ask us to think about the necessary distinction between the work and the book. This is a distinction that the poet herself has always insisted that we attend to, as readers. In her essay, "Poems are not meant to lay still," she begins with the assertion that "because words don't (always) need pages, I have published extensively through readings, performances and recordings. I have been reluctant to commit my poetry to the page over the years because, for the most part these poems are not meant to lay still" (Allen 1995, 253). In editing this volume, Allen's numerous reflections on the complex relationship between the poem and the book have been foremost in my mind. This ambivalence about the book as a primary artifact of the poetic word should also inform readers' approach to this volume.

Make the World New brings together some of the highlights of Lillian Allen's work. While this volume revisits well-known poems from her books *Rhythm an' Hardtimes* (1982), *Women Do This Every Day* (1993), and *Psychic Unrest* (1999), as well as assembling new and previously uncollected poems, there is also Allen's rich publication history of sound recordings. These include two Juno Award-winning albums, *Revolutionary Tea Party* (1985) and *Conditions Critical* (1987), along with her other albums such as *Freedom & Dance* (1999) and *Anxiety* (2012), which cannot be adequately represented in a collection such as this. Many of these poetry recordings have entered Canadian mainstream popular culture. However, less known are Lillian Allen's writings for children, which appear in volumes such as *Why Me?* (1991) and *Nothing But A Hero* (1992). These certainly deserve greater consideration and republication. Meaningful attention to Allen's verse for children might lead to more complex examinations of her interlinked roles as poet, feminist, mother, grandmother, activist, public intellectual, and educator. The limited space afforded by a slim volume such as this has meant that this aspect of her work could not be represented here, even as a few of the poems, such as "To the Child," "Trust," and "Jamaica - I Remember," engage with representations of childhood. This book then should not be read as the definitive collection of Allen's work. Rather, my experience in editing this volume has taught me the important lesson that such a collection may not be ultimately desirable or even possible.

We might understand this impossibility specifically in relation to Allen's artistic practice as a dub poet. As Mervyn Morris notes, "the ideal context for dub poetry is the live performance, it also makes itself available in various other ways: on radio, on television, in audio recordings, video recordings and on film. Many dub poets also publish books" (1999, 36). Morris's discussion of dub poetry, much like Lillian Allen's own reflections on the publication of her work, is keenly attentive to some of the same questions about venues and forms. In both Allen's and Morris's reflections, it is noteworthy that the printed poem is not the privileged text but, in fact, is listed last in each instance. Yet, as Morris also usefully reminds us, "because the best performance poets are poets, and the dance of language is central to what they do. To read their words with attention is often to be rewarded" (1999, 50). In the conversations that I have had with Lillian Allen, I have been constantly reminded of how much care and precision poets who publish their work as sound take when committing words to the page. What is produced is not simply a transcription and there is always an awareness of the need to make the poem resonate in multiple ways. Furthermore, this movement between what Allen calls "the life of a sound" (1993, 8) and its rendering or composition as lines on a page also inspires a self-conscious dimension that can be seen in dub poets' contemplations about the very nature of poetry. This is perhaps best evidenced by a range of metapoetic verse which take up reflections on poetry itself as a theme. Poems such as "The Poetry of Things," "PO E 3," "One Poem Town," "A Poem Against Things," and the final poem in this volume, "Dis Word," consciously interrogate our understandings of poetry and also raise questions about what poetry can do in the world.

The simultaneous challenge to, and expansion of, poetic possibility that is performed in Allen's work, has demanded of literary critics rich and nuanced ways of talking about her poetry as well as the development of an intriguing set of critical terms. Maria Caridad Casas has elaborated the idea of multimodality as a particular way of exploring how Allen's verse engages "the performance of a social position outside the written standard" (2009, 192). In outlining what he terms a reggae aesthetic, Kwame Dawes has also listed Allen among the poets "who have explicitly located their poetic instincts in reggae" (1999, 242). Susan Gingell, in her work, has used the concept of "see–hear asthetics" to signal an interrelated "reliance on *sounded* words as well as *printed* ones" and to give attention to some of Allen's textualizing practices (2009, 34, emphasis in original). The context of her examination of these aesthetics firmly situates Allen's work and words within the decolonial, poetic, and political legacies of the popular Jamaican poet Louise Bennett. Michael Bucknor, also attending to the complex relationship between the visual and the sonic possibilities of Allen's verse, has forwarded the notion of "body–memory poetics" to account for, among other things, the ways in which "Allen's material text in terms of its graphic configuration, aural structure and spatial arrangement recomposes the oral within the scribal" (1998, 303). For Bucknor, encounters with Allen's work demand the "negotation of not only the gaps between oral and scribal, but also between representation and object world, discourse and materiality, text and body" (1998, 303). This question of encounters as central to an understanding of dub praxis is further explored in Phanuel Antwi's examination of dub as "Black Atlantic Body-Archive" and as "sound archive" (2015, 70). Antwi's work usefully offers the concept of dub phenomenology to call attention to how "phenomenology and dub poetry share concepts and ideas on embodiment, reflectivity, situatedness, habit, and lived experience" (2015, 70). These critics variously engage with the s/pacing of Allen's words in sound, scribal, social, and performance con/texts and write about Allen's art in ways that usefully position the artist in dialogue with community. They remind us of Lillian Allen's assertion, at the end of the introduction to *Women Do This Every Day*, that "we made art part and parcel of political work" (1993, 21).

We must additionally recognize that this attention to art as praxis and as political work is also a Black feminist ethic of collective care. In this volume, the poems "Nellie Belly Swelly," "My Momma," "Marriage," "Feminism 101," and "Good Woman (Censorship)" all attend to the intergenerational experiences of women within patriarchy. There is also keen attention to gender in intersectional terms. For example, "Queenie Queenie and the Fall of Colonial Empire," which opens this collection, carefully juxtaposes the queen as a celebrated figure of womanhood with "likkle Delveena, nine years [...] a pickney wid a tough constitution, strong like a harse, full of she-self wid a mind of her own [...] and others, so many nice nice grandmothers and aunties." The poem uses the scene of a parade, occasioned by the queen's visit and with all in attendance, to ask us to reflect on the query, Delveena and her friends raise: "that dis one ooman, the queen, was getting so much attention." The poem offers a fascinating narrative return to Allen's previous articulation of the need to make "specific connections between oppression of women and imperialism" (1993, 19).

An understanding of these poems as complexly situated in relation to the world around us also demands that we think about the shifting meaning and context of these poems as they come into republication. We might thus think about what it means to revisit and reread a poem like "Nellie Belly Swelly," which foregrounds a young girl's sexual abuse, but which was written and published before the public discourse of the #MeToo movement. The case of the shifting resonances of the poem "Birth" is also instructive. Despite my initial introduction to Lillian Allen's work in the early 2000s, the first time I heard her read in a live performance was in

December 2014, at an event in Toronto, marking the 30th anniversary of her album *Revolutionary Tea Party*. This reading was convened in the wake of a summer in which there had been numerous and recurring incidents of police and state violence against Black people. The most reported of these at the time was the death of Eric Garner, who was choked to death by NYPD officers.[5] The event in Toronto happened only a week after the Richmond County grand jury decided not to indict the two NYPD officers implicated in Garner's death. In that context, Lillian Allen's reading of "Birth" took on new echoes. The poem is constructed as a series of labored breathing sounds. And in the space between breaths, as the audience listened, the poet softly pronounced the words, "I can't breathe." With this simple and poignant addition, which recalled Garner's last words (that had by then become a rallying cry for protestors calling for racial justice in the streets of cities across North America and beyond), the resonance of the poem had moved beyond birth sound/song. In a moment, the line between birth and death, and the arc of possibility of the Black body, was distilled as breath.

The words "can't breathe" have now become part of the published poem. In keeping with Allen's articulation of a poem as a living, breathing text (which is "not meant to lay still"), the version of "Birth" which appears in this volume revises the 1993 published version which appeared in *Women Do This Every Day*. It is also useful to note that the 1993 version, in turn, was a revision of "Birth Poem," which appeared on the album *Revolutionary Tea Party* accompanied by the dub(bed) track "Birth Version." The compelling thing about Allen's revision here is its allusiveness. Her dubbing of the phrase "can't breathe" echoes the circumstances of the death of Eric Garner, and more recently that of George Floyd, who was killed by Minneapolis police in May 2020 as he repeatedly uttered those words. But her allusion doesn't fix the resonances of the poem to those contexts or these scenes of Black death. Central to the poem is still an important writing of a gendered practice of making life. The poem notably ends with the word "breathe". Additionally, if we consider Phanuel Antwi's insightful reading of the poem "Birth" in "its textualized print form," in *Women Do This Every Day* as arranged into "the shape of a pregnant woman's belly" then Allen's revision here, in its layout, might meaningfully be read as extending that "sound portrait" (2015, 81). While the previously published version ends with the words "she born," here Allen offers us a second movement of the poem which also repeats the shape of a pregnant woman's belly. This second movement inscribes a distinctly cyclical dimension to the poem. If dub, in its aural arrangement and performance, is structured through a practice of repetition, Allen also uses the textual resources of the page to enact a particular mode of repetition as part of the writing of the intergenerationality that marks "Birth."

Yet these transformations and shifting resonances are not just about rewritings. They are also about rereadings. The completion of this volume amidst the COVID-19 global pandemic and in the aftermath of the 2020 summer of Black collective protests against racial injustice and police violence and which also saw toppling of a number of colonial monuments, will no doubt transform the ways in which these poems are read and re-read. For instance, Allen's poetry of orchestrated breathing, in this moment, becomes embodied resistance as well as a spiritual and practical reaffirmation of life. We might also think about how the poem "Birth" becomes echoed in her new poem "Pandemic." Much like "Birth," it contains instructions for collective breathing as a form of survival:

As we held our breath
Didn't breathe   until

In a collective gasp
we found a voice
to exhale

We can recognize then that the compilation of a volume of selected poems is not simply an act of gathering the poems. It is also a recontextualization of the work. In this volume, I have chosen to group the poems not according to the order of the texts in which they were originally published. Instead, a consideration of thematic connections and relations has guided the organization of this book. This allows for the mapping of continuities and connections between and across different poems, and will no doubt prove interesting for long-time readers and scholars of Lillian Allen's work.

The poems collected here do not simply range across different moments of Lillian Allen's career; they also bring together different geographies of the Black diaspora and different sites and spaces of revolutionary struggle. Poems like "In These Canadian Bones" reflect on Black and Indigenous relations, solidarities, and dispossessions. While the Laurier Poetry Series, in which this volume appears, focuses on the work of contemporary Canadian poets, it is also important to remember the transnational intimacies, scope, and resonances of Allen's poetry. Allen consistently reminds us of this in her explicit and deliberate claiming of the Jamaican poet, Louise Bennett, as literary foremother as well as in her referencing of the impact of the 1960s with its political and artistic convergences as seen in "the Black Power movement in America and its poets of resistance (Jane Cortez, Sonja Sanchez, Nikki Giovanni, Gil Scott-Heron, Amiri Baraka, The Last Poets and so on); the liberation from British colonial powers ... and the rise of the Rastafarian movement, emphasizing Black people's role in history, and a return to African roots" (1993, 13–14). Her work offers a challenge to fixed imaginings of bounded national traditions and asks us to think with more complexity about the very construction of these and about narrative frameworks of diaspora. She reminds me, for instance, of how she is simultaneously read as "foreign" in relation to the literary traditions of both Canada and Jamaica.

We also see this transnational and international sensibility in her careful mapping of the ways in which the emergence and development of dub poetry in Toronto must be considered in relation to Jamaica and to England and to the work of a generation of poets including "Oku Onuora, Mutabaruka, Jean Binta Breeze, Mikey Smith, Nabby Natural, Malachi Smith, Poets in Unity among others" (Allen 1993, 15). The poems which open this volume, "Queenie Queenie and the Fall of Colonial Empire," "Trust," and "JAMAICA - I Remember," recall and reflect on life in Jamaica. They each also subversively re-narrate a previous moment in Jamaica's history as a "history from below," or rather, they engage a practice of what Louise Bennett has termed "[turning] history upside dung!" (1982, 106). By this, I mean that these poems foreground the voices, lives, experiences, and sensibilities of the working class as a site from which to critique dominant histories of post-colonial becoming. They remind us of Lillian Allen's astute assertion that among the "contributions of dub poetry to our society" has been "engendering working class solidarity," "disrupting established discourse" and the "expansion and democratization of categories of both poet and audience" (2014, n.p.). Yet, while these poems offer undoubtedly loving portraits, they also refuse easy nostalgia. We should read them as mobilizing both language and feeling as part of a fundamental critique of the discourses and paradigms of development that structure our capitalist present. While this collection opens with poems of Jamaican life, we also observe Lillian Allen as a poet concerned with freedom, survival, and change across the world. There are poems collected here about Nicaragua, Haiti, South Africa, the US, and Canada. These poems also write specific cities and communities into Black diasporic memory, such as her writing of the urban Toronto community of Regent Park in the poem "Rub A Dub Style Inna Regent Park" and Jane and Finch in the poem "Dark Winds."

This transnational vision is also the context for the call to "make the world new." The title of this book takes a line from the poem "Nicaragua." Like several other poems collected in this volume, it speaks about the possibilities for social and political change glimpsed at different sites of resistance in the long history of the twentieth century. The poem is reflective of Lillian Allen's wider body of work in which the narration and interrogation of specific sites of struggle become intertwined with a greater visioning of revolutionary possibility. As Allen writes, "there is a spirit that unites us in *revolution*." This awareness of revolution as a shared legacy, for those whom Frantz Fanon (1963) has called "the wretched of the earth," combines with the poet's writing of revolution—the will to change the world—as something that bubbles up from the soul of a people but which is also nurtured through poetry and its attention to struggle, at the level of discourse as well as politics.

> There is a watering hole
> way in the souls of men and women
> who dare to sstt—struggle
> (uggle to struggle to uggle to struggle)

Allen's poem brings together multiple resonances of the phrase "make the world new." It becomes linked to what the poem's speaker calls the possibilities of "another language," but also "another intention"—a new political will—as well as "another story"—a call to make and imagine new and different futures.

In remembering the early days of dub poetry, Lillian Allen has written that "The first generation of dub poets wrote of police brutality, of dashed immigrants' dreams, of hard work and little pay, of the oppression of Black women at the hands of Black men, of the need to nurture and fight back"(1993, 20–21). In reading these poems today, we might ask, how much has changed? The call to "make the world new" seems more urgent now than ever.

—*Ronald Cummings*

Notes

1 Personal correspondence with Faizal Deen, December 15, 2020.
2 Conversation with Nalini Mohabir, December 14, 2020.
3 I use the term arrivants here for a number of reasons. First it marks a literary kinship between the work of Lillian Allen and Kamau Brathwaite whose trilogy *The Arrivants* is a foundational work of New World poetry. Second, I draw on Jodi Byrd's work in *The Transit of Empire* where she reflects on *The Arrivants* as a text and a concept that might help us think through Black people's relationship to land and belonging in the Americas and might help us examine Indigenous and Black dispossession relationally within structures of settler colonialism.
4 Personal correspondence with Kaie Kellough, December 14, 2020.
5 His death was ruled as a homicide by the coroner.

Works Cited

Allen, Lillian. *Anxiety*. Toronto: Verse to Vinyl, 2012.
———. "Assessing Dub Poetry's Literary Impact-Black Voice," Anne Szumigalski Memorial Lecture – League of Canadian Poets AGM. 6 June 2014. https://lillian allen.ca/blog/
———. *Conditions Critical*. (L.P). Toronto: Verse to Vinyl, 1987.
———. *Freedom & Dance*. (L.P). Toronto: Verse to Vinyl, 1999.
———. *Nothing But A Hero*. Toronto: Well Versed Publications, 1992
———. "Poems are not meant to lay still" *The Other Woman: Women of Colour in Contemporary Canadian Literature*. Ed. Makeda Silvera. Toronto: Sister Vision Press, 1995, 253–62.
———. *Psychic Unrest*. Toronto: Insomniac Press, 1999.
———. *Revolutionary Tea Party*. (L.P). Toronto: Verse to Vinyl, 1985.
———. *Rhythm an' Hardtimes*. Toronto: Domestic Bliss Publishers/Flash Frontline Publications, 1982.
———. *Why Me?* Toronto: Well Versed Publications, 1991.
———. *Women Do This Every Day*. Toronto: Women's Press, 1993.
Antwi, Phanuel. "Dub Poetry as a Black Atlantic Body-Archive." *Small Axe* 19.3 (2015): 65–83.
Bennett, Louise. *Selected Poems*. Kingston: Sangster, 1982.
Brathwaite, Kamau. *The Arrivants*. Oxford: Oxford University Press, 1973.
Bucknor, Michael. "Body-Vibes: (S)pacing the Performance in Lillian Allen's Dub Poetry." *Thamyris*, 5/2, (1998): 301-322.
Byrd, Jodi. *The Transit of Empire: Indigenous Critiques of Colonialism*. Minneapolis: University of Minnesota Press, 2011.
Caridad Casas, Maria. *Multimodality in Canadian Black Feminist Writing: Orality and the Body in the Work of Harris, Philip, Allen and Brand*. Amsterdam and New York: Rodopi, 2009.

Dawes, Kwame. *Natural Mysticism: Towards a New Reggae Aesthetic.* Leeds: Peepal Tree Press, 1999.

Fanon, Frantz. *The Wretched of the Earth.* New York: Grove Weidenfeld, 1963.

Gingell, Susan. "Coming Home through Sound: See–Hear Aesthetics in the Poetry of Louise Bennett and Canadian Dub Poets," *Journal of West Indian Literature* 17.2 (2009): 32–48.

Morris, Mervyn. *Is English We Speaking and other essays.* Kingston: Ian Randle Publishers, 1999.

Queenie Queenie and the Fall of Colonial Empire

A whole year de people dem spend a fix-up and a prepare fah her Royal Imperial Majectic, Queen of England to visit the town of St Jago de La Vega, the second largest city on the island of Jamaica. In this likkle town de people dem wuk hard an' make de La Vega a pleasurable place fi dem an' dem family and near-family, cause anybody de bout is family.

Not nuff industry of employ except the textile mill, miles up Ariguanabo near Bog Walk. An' there was Caymanas sugar estate factory on the road to old Port Henderson wid marble statue of Admiral Lord Nelson standing in fa de Queen and conquest. Yu wouda did lucky if one of yu distant relative or even third cousin removed did get a job dey. An' yes, the coveted Alcan job uppa Lindstead. If you or fambily member get that job, yu done dead and find yu self a heaven. Dat there was red golden. But it sad how dem dig up the ground, whole side a mountain, mash it down, strip up Massa God earth, then mush it up with caustic soda, and move wey de humble vendors and hardworking small farmer fambily dem. Dem tek wey dem want and sen big fat tanker ship loads to Canada and America to refine (an' doan get mi started on that, like we only good enough fi so-so dirt and not refinement!). Dem leave the mountain valley of caustic soda sludge, a constipated red river bringing sadness and ill-health. Otherwise is so-so penny hustling, hand to mouth work at Record Office, or fi the more tapanaris dem with connection, wuk at Parish Council. Prisons, yes; warder work, police, hospital, school teecha, learn trade, rum shop, dry goods store haberdashery, small grocers, or wuk at the market or cemetery; Number Five Bawling Ground. Days-wuk, domestic, any likkle ting.

Hand mi downs, recycle, pull an stretch, one-one coco. Every mikkle mek a mukkle and every mukkle mek a mite. Day in day out. One-one coco full basket.

* * * * *

In the town, likkle Delveena, nine years and swish young was a pickney wid a tough constitution, strong like a harse, full of she-self wid a mind of her own. She an' her friend dem couldn't understand wey all the fus 'bout this visit and why when there are so many gazillion people in the world, heroes and sheroes who do so much for human-kind, so many who do kind things for dem neighbours and others, so many nice-nice grandmothers and aunties, that dis one ooman, the queen, was getting so much attention.

All the likkle pickney dem inna the town of St Jago de la Vega was well verse pon the Queen, her Empire and her riches. De pickney dem was made to practice day-in day-out on how to behave in front of Royalty. These here pickney dem was no flenky-flenky pickney. Dem was haughty and used to run up and down inna hot-hot sunshine plenty. But none of dem ever was stretch to the limits like them was the day the Queen of England came to visit Jamaica. Imagine all the pickney dem inna the broiling tropical sun all day ah wait fi get a glimpse of the Queen of England as if she couda did save dem soul.

Sun set an' sun rise, people wuk an' pot bwoil. Dem no wait, dem no hurry, time run come in front of dem to bring this day. Blaaps! The poor likkle pickney dem was scrubbed down, cleaned behind the ears and under dem arm and scrubbed double in hidden creases. All dem poverty and lack of opportunity fi a bright future covered up under the sheen of polished shoes, powdered faces and impeccably starched and ironed uniforms. Crisp an' not a crease.

De pickney dem was herded like cattle and put pon show fi assure the Queen that her loyal subjects will forever be reproducing likkle loyal subjects, if she don't object, that is.

* * * * *

Dis ya visit was the biggest sinting de town ever see. The biggest sinting the whole island ever see for that matter. Joe Blowwow who sell scrapses meat reduce im price. Miss Dina sweep up her yard and tie bow pon the guinep tree. Miss Meeme spend two days straight without a drop a sleep and mek greata-cake like it was a did go out a style. Even at the Chinaman shop dem spruce up the place and ah give wey free sweetie to the school children dem. Everybody dress-up dem house or one room like is Easter and Christmas in one. The nice-nice tablecloth, chenille spread and bleach clean curtain wey only see the light of day fi very special occasions, proudly displayed to welcome the Queen. De way everybody dah gwan, yu wouda did think sey a Christ a come again.

Buzz, buzz, buzzing. De word was buzzing; Britannia. "Britannia Britannia rules the waves and Britons never never never will be a slave!" This sentiment was drilled into every likkle pickney and into every woman and man in the country for a whole year. Rule Britannia! Well, well, Mother Thelma did sey dem a trow dem wud pon Black people, cause if dem invent slavery and dem will never, never, never (not one or two but three "never" be a slave), then a who fi be the slave?

For the entire year in the town of de la Vega, the word Britannia ruled supreme and was a rallying call. Britannia was represented by her stately self the Queen, England, the Empire, and the universe.

* * * * *

Hurried, harried, hassled, and whipped into shape. That's how it wouda did look to you if you did see how dem pack dat town square overflowing with school pickney, all in line and formation more orderly than the eleventh battalion of the Queen's very army. All this by eight am sharp that morning. All to dutiful await the visitation of her Imperial Majesty, Queen Elizabeth the second of England.

Bacchanalia throughout the town that day. Military bands, police, and boys scout groups march up and down through the streets. Hundreds of little British flags waved everywhere. Big flags were on every flagpole in schools, prisons, churches, and public places. And choruses of 'Rule Britannia' could be heard every whey yu turn.

It was said that from dem hear the word 'go' over a year ago, the ole soljah man dem deck out dem-self inna full soljah uniforms wid dem ribbons, dem buttons, dem swashes and dem medals, and dem practice march up and down and around the town five nights a week. Proud sey till! Dem talk story and tell bout soljah life and wartime happenings. Dem was like survivors of Battleship Galaxia Star War attack awaiting their rightful accolades from the Devine leader of the universe, though nuff-nuff ah dem never even been to Up Park Camp or see no war business, ongle the uniform.

* * * * *

People rush to finish tidy-up dem house before the sun come up. Dem bring out the cup an' saucers dem nevah touch fi years, just in case. Nuff a de church people dem recall scriptures an de Easter song about Zacchaeus that goes, "Now Zacchaeus was a very little man and a very little man was he. He climbed up into the sycamore tree for the Saviour he wanted to see (repeat chorus) for the Saviour he wanted to see." And as the Saviour passes by he looked up in the tree, and said; "Now Zacchaeus, you come down, I'm coming to your house for tea, I'm coming to your house for tea." Oh lordie, lord!

The route da the Queen was to take was all fixed-up, bruk-down fence, mash-up wall, and some yard wey never cleanup ebber. Everybody was given freebie government paint and materials to do repairs and all the neighbours worked together with even the government man dem giving a hand to do a splendid facelift job. The way the place look refreshing it mek some people remark; "…mek dem government man couldn't help we out just fi wi-self sometimes. De ongle time dem do something fi wi is when dem waan wi vote or dem waan show aff to foreigner!"

* * * * *

Don't get it wrong now. Is not everybody did feel subjected to the Queen. Nuff people gather round and backstab she. Dem wonder out loud why if she is the richest woman in the world and control so much wealth and riches, why she sending only so-so sympathy to the poor in her Christmas message, when all she have to do is to get up offa some of that cash?

A group of Rasta man led by Bongo George and Count Roots draft up a letter wey sey "the reason the Queen have up so much money is because she tief up the treasures of Africa and nuff other countries, and tief up peoples land wey dem own and live pon continuously long before she or anybody she know or related to was ever born…" And dem demand that she giv the monies, treasures and lands back. But when dem tek the letter to the authorities to ask it to be delivered to the Queen, dem arrest every single one of dem wid signature pon the letter and threaten Bongo George and Count Roots with the Cat o' Nine. And dem never let the Rasta man-dem outta jail till the Queen was 'safely out of the Caribbean'. And when dem finally let dem out, dem dreadlocks cut off clean-clean, and the Official dem give dem each a likkle paper bag wid dem personal souvenir of the Queen's visit. Each bag haveen some tough red an' white sweetie, Union Jack stickers, and pictures of the Queen and the Royal Family.

* * * * *

Thousands lined the street with the motorcade on its way. The pickney dem wait patiently from way before eight o clock in Massa God mawning. Dem bear up like highly trained troopers. Dem couldn' even talk or go pee-pee. As soon as yu hear a likkle susu, a big mouth teacher wouda did yell out; "Be quiet, please! Respect for the Queen!" The pickney dem just strups up dem teeth and stan up dey wid de patience of Job. For hours dem pack together inna the blazing sun, though not as tight as bodies pon a human cargo ship. When eleven 'o' clock come, it was like the sun was full of vengeance. If it couda did talk a pure blirdeets it wouda did sey, the hot sun that is. Instead, the sun blaze down mercilessly pon the pickney dem. In the meantime, the teacher dem wouda spell dem one anada off and go rest off inna the shade, wey dem sip likkle Kool-Aid sweeten wid brown sugar. Officials of pure so-so big time, full belly man dem sit reverentially pon the platform that was build specially for the occasion by the undertaker carpenter son, Walley. De man dem siddown stiff and compliant, well pleased with the world. Only intermittently dem oulda fan flies and whisper kindly to each other like dem feeling a magic.

* * * * *

Bam bla daps bam! At eleven-thirty, the sun claimed its first victim.

The nine-year-old Delveena just couldn't tek it no more. She was the first to hit the pavement. An' then a wave of fainting spell see dozens of shiny Black children been taken into the shade and fanned, smelling sauced and bay-rummed. The blazing sun was the only sinting that showed no sign of tiring. Everybody look wilted. Even the flag stap flutter pon the flagpole looking thirsty fi wata. By twelve-forty-five even the die-hard loyalist was starting to turn irritated, albeit with a slight stoicism. But they were not nearly as irritated as irate parents proudly watching from the other side of the town's square who declared that; 'the Queen didn't care a hoot bout dem pickney dem wey a bun up inna the boiling heat' because, as soft-spoken Dina reasoned out loud, "…if it was fi she pickney, Prince this and Princess that, she wouda did have servants a fan them an' hold umbrella over them head!"

At one-thirty pm a small breeze fluttered through the crowd. Tensions eased, and before you could sey; 'Jack Mandora mi nuh choose none', a woo of excitement went up to welcome the queen. It was like magic. A beautiful angelic wave-like chorus of woos floated up over the gathering of ten thousand dutifully gathered subjects. And then there was silence… and confusion. What was supposed to be the Queen appeared in a white convertible without crown, throne, horses or foots-men. A person who appeared to be the Queen waved tiredly with one hand. Slowly. Children turned and searched the eyes of each other, in confusion to see and ask-ing 'where is the Queen?' There were no clues to signify that this tired looking white lady with a waving hand was the Queen. The pickney dem strain dem neck while the Queen was in full view, still looking, still asking; "Where is the Queen? Where is the Queen?" People start to strups up dem teeth, vex soh till. After all dem preparations and excitement the Queen didn't even have the courtesy to show up in her Crown. Bad enough she didn't bring any of the postcard looking guards in front of Buckingham Palace, and not even one of Princess Anne's dress-up horse.

The boiling sun eased its persistence. King's House, the court house building, Parish Council and Record Office with the Rodney statue part, threw a gentle shadow like a sign that the universe and Jah know that de pickney dem couldn't tek the heat nuhmore. The convertible carrying the queen and her motorcade came to a stop right in front of the platform full of politicians, government officials, dignitaries and rich people. All the man dem pon the platform get up in unison and give the Queen a serious salute. The mayor with a necklace straight-outta-Compton presented the Queen with a key to the town. Strups-strups an' strups up was heard all around. Some people say dem was going home that night to change the lock pon them door.

* * * * *

In the shade by the side of the platform away from hoards of uniformed tired school children, likkle Delveena was recovering from her faint. She looked up and saw an ordinary looking white person. She asked to make sure, A dat the Queen? A she dat? A de Queen dat? The teacher beside Delveena shussh her down to indicate for her to be quiet and then replied with tremendous excitement, "Yes that is she. That is wi Queen!"

Delveena eased herself up from where the teacher had put her to rest. She looked around from left to right, at all the other pickney dem and all the other nuff-nuff people who dress up demselves pretty like puss. She looked at the tapanaris people dem pon the platform and hedged, then darted to the convertible that carried the Queen. She stood beside the convertible, the Queen still waving to the crowd. The likkle Delveena put her hands pon kimbo, push out her chest and shouted; "Look mi prettier than de Queen!" A loud cheer went up in the Town's square. The teacher strode embarrassingly and grab the likkle Delveena, and hauled her to the back of the platform where another teacher held her to the ground. The Queen didn't even blink. She just kept waving her arm in slow motion as she looked straight into the crowd. She seemed disinterested and fatigued, growing more tired by the second. Her waving arm moving even slower through the thickness of the tropical heat. Within moments her motorcade drove on.

The Queen had come and gone, just like that.

* * * * *

In the meantime, Delveena escaped the teacher who was holding her to the ground. She ran out into the crowd. The crowd went wild with cheering her. They lifted her up in the air. The other school children jumped around and clapped and tussled jokingly with each other forgetting their dozens of rehearsals on how to vacate the Square in an orderly manner.

Teachers yelled for order and quiet without effect. The authorities came over the loudspeaker calling for quiet and order. People carried on with their chatter and jovialities as if an inside damn had broken loose. No one paid attention to the high-pitched calls for quiet and order that continued over the public address system for some time. A festival atmosphere erupted.

* * * * *

Afterwards, the town buzzed with festivities, thousands more little British flags and pictures of the Queen appeared everywhere. Souvenirs of American made British sweets, and pens, pencils, and exercise books made in Japan were being distributed freely. Not long after, a light dusk came and brought a dreamy atmosphere.

There were big questions on everybody's lip. The questions and answering became a game. Someone would take on the role of the questioner in a group and the whole group would provide the answer. It was done kinda sing-songy with a beat.

"Did   you   see   the   queen?"
The   answer;   "Which   queen?"
Then,   "Was   she   big   or   was   she   little?"
The   answer;   "She   was   likkle   with   mukkle   an'   mettle!"
"Was   she   wrong   or   was   she   right?"

The answer; "Who cares. She showed some life!"

The nine-year-old Delveena was unofficially crowned 'de la Vega's little queen' and was nicknamed Queenie-Queenie.

After a year of anticipation and preparations, the Queen of England, Her Imperial Majestic Royal Elizabeth de Second had come and gone. Somehow her status had slipped, forever. It was no wonder that the fate of her empire would follow suit.

Trust

Who can we trust? Whose words will rescue us?

When I was growing up in Spanish Town Jamaica, **people had** two different types of **currencies** in conducting **commerce**; you could pay in cash for something or you could **trust** it. "Mi madah sen' mi fi **trust** a loaf of harddough bread and some **butter** 'till Friday." Trust was a popular currency and **transactional and relational**; the way it should be. In some communities it was more popular than cash. Trust was **metaphysical** in the way that it moved through space and time to **materialize** goods to sustain life. There was a rhythm and recurrence to the cycle of trust and predictability to the **promise** of payment. For these folks, the shopkeeper would just make a mental note. For those who had a harder time of meeting their basic needs, the shopkeeper would keep a kind of ledger. It was such an **honour** system that those who were on rock-hard times and couldn't deliver on the promise to pay, were cause for great **sympathy** and even charity. What was owed would be suspended indefinitely or simply forgiven and in **addition** they would be given what they needed for free. If you messed up, the consequences were great. Simply, you would not be given any more **credit**; your currency of trust could not be used again for anything or with anyone. You felt ashamed. There was an **instinct** that told you that you were part of an **ecosystem** and you had **damaged** it.

In a rum shop where trust had been broken, a sign warned; "In God We Trust, All Others Pay Cash".

I remember a time when a person was as **good** as their word as a **societal norm**. Our need to trust and be trusted was once **fundamental** to who we are as **individuals** and as a **society**. **Accountability** was a badge of honour. I would venture to say that between immoral **priests**, crooked **politicians** and **falsehood** in advertisements, the **public** notion of trust took a **beating**. And not to overlook **dishounourable** authority figures, **unconscionable** greed of business cultures, the **Madoffs of the world**, **alternative facts**, and the all too commonplace Hydro-One type debacles further impugning notions of public trust and **normalizing** its demise. The **private** notions were always complicated and contested, what with the rate of **infidelity**, incest and sexual abuse all from the very **people** one should trust the most. A loss of private and public trust is **psychic abuse**.

I am reminded of an anecdote of a man who had fallen down a cliff and had grabbed onto and hung from a branch of a jotting root, **dangling** above jagged rocks. He pleaded; "God, I know you're up there. I have complete trust in you, please tell me what to do." After a short electric pause a **god-like** voice boomed back, "Yes, son it's me God, just relax and let go. You're gonna be alright."
The man glanced down at the eager jaggedness of rocks dozens of feet below then frightfully tightened his grip and shouted in an **existential,** desperate tone;
"Hey, is **anybody else** up there?"

In some ways, I think that is where **we** are in **the world** today.

JAMAICA – I Remember

Sunday evening breeze
Rice an' peas, roast pork and chicken curry
We change from our Sunday school best
Frilled socks turned so delicately down
Bata cha–cha-cha soulfully brushed to sparkle
The crepe- canvas' perfect white
Grinning in the Sunday evening light

We pack up a canteen Thermos
Four medium-sized tin can   hooked together
Swing pon each other like a Jacob's ladder
Parboiled an' red beans, chicken back in yellow grease
Okra, ground provisions
Dinner for granny-auntie-cousin Lovie-Hilda
Down the lane beside Phillipo Baptist Church
French Street corner Spanish Town
close to Russian shop 'cross from the Chiney man store
Where the East Indian family grows callaloo next door

So abundant tall the guinep tree shadows
Ever blooming limes and a small Susumber grove
Through banging broken wooden gate where the cistern hides
Its pipe drip   drips   drips   dripping
No matter how hard you tighten
The trick --lock it off slight, just right, slow down, quiet
Tip away   *sh -ssh -ssshhh*
Or else it pours again to dance brushed-green
Slime oh so lazily on the iron gray of the cistern's concrete

And we children, one by one get out hugs
For granny-auntie-cousin Lovie-Hilda
Half blind, lovesome, a no-toothed smile
Soft wrinkles jiggle and ripple when sparked to laughter
How granny-auntie-cousin Lovie-Hilda got her name
I couldn't say, but it grew with her age

We light up her day, her very existence
We think her Gran Aunt with a proper G
Our Granny-Auntie-Cousin Lovie-Hilda
Not connected by blood or marriage

Or relatives in common
She was only a woman who way back when
A child in my Grandmother's childhood
Made blood by passing time.

Nellie Belly Swelly

Nellie was thirteen
don't care 'bout no fellow
growing in the garden
among the wild flowers

she Mumma she dig & she plant
nurtures her sod
tends her rose bush
in the garden pod

lust leap the garden fence
pluck the rose bud
bruk it ina the stem

oh no please no
was no self defense
oh no please no
without pretence
offered no defense
to a little little girl
called Nellie

Nellie couldn't understand
Mr. Thompson's hood
so harsh, so wrong
in such an offensive

Nellie plead, Nellie beg
Nellie plead, Nellie beg
but Mr. Thompson's hood
went right through her legs

knowing eyes blamed her

Nellie disappeared from sight
news spread wide
as the months went by
psst psst psst Nellie belly swelly
Nellie belly swelly Nellie belly swelly
children skipped to Nellie's shame

Nellie returned from the night
gave up her dolls
and the rose bush died
Nellie Momma cried, Nellie Momma cried
her little Nellie no more child again

No sentence was passed
on this menacing ass
who plundered Nellie's childhood

In her little tiny heart
Nellie understood war

She mustered an army within her
strengthened her defence
and mined the garden fence

No band made a roll
skies didn't part
for this new dawn
infact, nothing heralded it
when this feminist was born

My Momma

When it came to being revolutionary
my Momma she stood up for us
she would fight off a bus

Papa breaks limits
screech skid marks in our minds
aiming to make ladies of us
hold us back in time

my sister Doreen she was greedy
and liked only girls
my father didn't mind
or thought nothing unkind
boys were too much like him
sadocentric and potent

my Momma she was pregnant every year or so
bore us twelve sibilies
six girls in a row
she scrubbed floors
washed and hung miles and miles of clothes
got pregnant again
my mother, pregnant was her biggest event

she left my father
for Kate Millett, Angela Davis, and the North Star
for the first time in her life

she would sing liberation
and live with it
            (swing low sweet chariot
                        step it 'gainst babylon)

my Momma she said freedom
was buying steak if she wanted
without asking anyone
It was wearing her skirt on her knees
or wherever she please
without displeasing someone

watching her children grow were the chains
that kept her bold and hoping
independence severed umbilicals
and released her

my Momma she watched us get married
and divorced
fall in and out of love
and stood by us

times we pass connect join
run rings 'round each other
slip in and out of time
umbilicals reconnect
knot
through her maternal line

my Momma she say
every woman has the experience of giving all she could
and every woman knows the feeling
of having nothing left
not even for herself
women were raised to be givers
darned if we are not good

my Momma she say
any woman who can make a dot into a child
inside of her
and bring it outside to us
is a model for a revolution

my Momma
when it comes to being revolutionary
she stood up for us
and beside us

she did always say
it takes two

Marriage

When mi sidown
pon mi bombo claat
inna calico dress
under the gwango tree
a suck coarse salt
fi the night fi dun
wen twist-face joan
an mi man mus come
down those concrete steps
from her tatch-roof house
han-in-han an smile
pon dem face

an it buss-up inna mi 'ead
Like cistern it flow
blood full mi yeye
ah tear im shut
rip 'im pride
the little heng-pon-nail

the two rocky miles 'ome
we drop some hiss
cuss soaked licks
kasha sticks

but later on
ah sooth 'im pain

bathe the bad-blood down
the cistern drain
ten common-law-years
inna wi tenement yard

an sure as 'ell
wi anger rest
'im eyes regret
plea 'an confess
then 'im glide mi
to gramma dead-lef bed
an' marry mi

under the chinnelle spread
again an' again
till day does done
evening come

Birth

(9 months out of the year a woman in labour,
if it was a man, I bet they woulda paid her)

an' mi labour   an' mi labour
an' mi labour   an' mi labour

ah a ah   ah a ah ah aa

ah a ah   ah a ah ah aaa

ah a   ah ah a ah ah aaaa

aha   aaaaa   ahaa

an' mi breathe   can't breathe
an' mi breathe   can't breathe

aha   aaaaaa

an baps

she born

an life yu see
how it nice yu see
how it rife yu see

aha aaaaa   ahaa

aaaaaa aah

aaah

breathe

To the Child

To the child who loves to sing silly songs
to the child who dresses a little weird
to the child whose heart wanders
for you I've written this poem

Not everyone can fit in a round or square
not every bird will sing a loud song
not every tree will outgrow another one
but every child can be someone

and to the child who can't always win a race
to the child who can't draw a perfect heart
to the child who has a weird little laugh
to the child who somehow stands apart

Broken

The boy is broken on the sidewalk
The sidewalk is broken beneath him
His colour is back (not black)
Because it was washed out
Worrisome for his aunt
Whose leg was taken to save her life
No, not diabetes but from shrapnel   Flying

What have we forgotten to say
to give the heart ease
just out of diapers learning to walk
the body seeks an inherent language of peace
What do you wish to be?
Happy, I'm sure

You may ask;
Whose voice is in my head, so fully formed?
So old and heavy with pain and venge
behind the lead(er) passage is set
funeral a badge

Language now frozen symbols
Symbols like bells calling
Calling to the divide
Fists and blows and broken
Splayed like shrapnel on the sidewalk

Fall away   fall away
What do you wish for the world
What do you wish for your heart
Boy broken on sidewalk
Sidewalk broken beneath boy

Conditions Critical

Dem a mash it up down inna Jamaica
dem a add it up down inna Jamaica
dem a mash it up down inna Jamaica
dem a add it up down inna Jamaica

gas prices bounce
hoops for the skies
a likkle spark and embers of oppression
rise
people tek to the streets
it's no negotiating stance

when do yu want freedom?
yesterday!
how do you propose you'll get it?
by the people's way!

soh, that's why …
dem a mash it up down inna Jamaica
dem a add it up down inna Jamaica

dem sey dem tired of trying to buy the country back
from the Americans and the IMF pact
a little friendly debt with an open end
it feel like the ball and chain game again

soh, that's why …
dem a mash it up down inna Jamaica
dem a add it up down inna Jamaica
conditions critical
freedom has been mythical

every few years years a new deliverer come
say 'better must come, let *me* lead the way my people'

seems better get delayed
somewhere hiding
it's quarter to twelve
an' it's getting late

better change to waiting
an' we waiting here a while
an' the weight
is piling on our backs
we sweating and dying
under disparity's attacks, attacks attacks

an' our children still bawling
our ancestors still calling
an' wi right ya soh demanding

so that's why ...
dem a mash it up down inna Jamaica
dem a add it up down inna Jamaica
conditions critical
freedom has been mythical
conditions critical

ecliptical
critical

Nicaragua

I can tell the flames of a secret fire
flaring Sandinista's courage
I can see in the darkened bushes
smell the freshness of an idea taking root
I can make my way through the darkness
looking is just *one* way to see

I can sense another language
another intention
another story that will tell itself
make the world new

There is something from this journey
makes me stand up
makes my legs strong

There is a watering hole
way in the souls of men and women
who dare to sstt -- struggle
(uggle to struggle to uggle to struggle)

There is a language that's universal
that's known through the ages
whispered in the streets
and shouted in houses
there is a spirit that unites us in *revolution*

I shall always remember yours days of bravery
and sadness
I shall always remember your joy
I shall always remember your deliberate
and spontaneous intentions
the love that flourishes in the souls of your people
Nicaragua
I shall always remember
I know

Dictator
(for Haiti)

the dust that makes you will someday
turn to mud in the rain
and fertilize the land for the peasants
its fruit shall bear no resemblance of you
only a song of the past about evil days
long gone
shall we remember your name
dictator

Could It Happen in America

It was 2029 in America
the great crowd stood by the wall
though it wasn't all that visible
it separated the rich from the poor
they stood and they said no more
in our time poverty must end
they shook and the rumblings
from the things that they said
the wall came tumbling down

could it happen
happen in America
could the people file free in the streets
could we impeach the entire congress
could the voiceless now speak
could we reorganize the political system
to meet each and every need
could the poor see prosperity in America
and could we all be free

could it happen
happen in America
could the walls come tumbling down
could it happen in our lifetime
could we do it, our wills, our sound
could we march through the streets
could we stand by the wall
could we all be there and sounding the call

could it happen
happen in America
could the wall of poverty fall

The Wait of History

in the dawning of a golden day
in a schizophrenia
an alienation mushrooms

a river of hope
reality like a ghost
the snail pace of history

how could it be that no one goes to jail
for the crime Apartheid

we can forgive but not excuse
set in their old ways
pillage and privilege die hard
if not exorcised decisively

words of freedom
words of reconciliation
words words words
language is a militia

the sound of wait falls in the forest
the grey nothingness of appearances and systemics
a greater silence than prayer

in a schizophrenia
in the clanking rust slow turning wheels
equality is a bounced cheque
stamped justice
cash withdrawn by a few

Song for Newfoundland

The pace of unfolding Newfoundland's life
connects to my own
though I am Caribbean in North American clime
I could make Newfoundland my home

Language swirl of the Newfoundlander's roll
where syllables greet each other
as if long-lost cousins
hold and embrace   slip   flip
slide away
where word rhythms sway
make the voice rise   sing
twist and play

It is here in the family of heart rhythms
and soul beats
a great big wall-less place
where the letter "h" disappears
for a well deserved vacation
somewhere between language and music
in a mystical twilight haze
I found my connection
Newfoundland's soul

Rasta in Court

Listen to the sound an' the beat of yu heart
Listen to the rebels an' the Rasta dem a talk
Listen to them chanting... listen to dem rapping
Listen to the shifting of the planet that is happening

The Rastaman check him bike
sey him haffi go down to Eglinton this night
ride him bike pon the sidewalk bright
bops to the left and weave to the right
dolly 'round the corner feeling very nice
'im ites green and gold flashing bold in the night
him hands off the handle bar of him bike
and before yu could sey "Hey Dreadie, everything alright?"
'im smash right into a policeman on patrol in the night

Oh what a fright   oh what a sight
Rastaman lying on top of a policeman with 'im bike
The policeman revive... jump up hypnotized
and promptly arrest the Rastaman man
for riding 'im bicycle without any light

Rastaman reply
"I am one of Jah Jah children
I and I got my light which is Jah-guide
so, dem can't come arrest I and I
'cause in Babylon there's no night"

As the law would have it
them went to court
As Rasta luck would get it
jury dope
strict stiff courtroom full
judge keen and jury dutiful
The Rastaman decide to defend himself
and present him case in full

First him call himself as a witness
(hear wey him sey now, 'him is Jah witness');
"Ma light your honour is in I eye
If I ride my bicycle when I eye shut

I couldn't did see nothing
no matter if there was a thousand light 'pon I bike
When Jah give light him give I and I, I sight
And I eyes was open
So yu honour, dem can't come sey
I and I was riding without any light"

So the Judge sey, "… ah… ah let me try and get it straight
Mr. whats-yu-name… Rastafari-you-and-you…? If your eyes
were closed there would be darkness, no light. But your eyes
were open so…… so that meant you had your light…
Ah see… Then how come you run into the policeman with
your bike?"

"Because, yu honour," Rastaman replied, "as there is dark-
ness… there is light. And if the policeman did have 'im
light, him oulda did see I"

Guilty or not guilty   a jury must decide

"… And further more yu honour," Rastaman chides,
"Only one man can judge I and that is Jah Rastafari, Selassie I"

The jury returned   split.   Verdict undecide
the judge had was to let the Rastaman slide
The policeman clutch him chest and started to cry

Rastaman jump 'pon him chariot of a bike
'im ites green and gold
flashing like a light
him bob anda weave and hear him as him ride…
"Mi light beside mi liver… and mi light in mi eye…
can't check sey I mon Rasta guilty
when from Jah I and I get I guide!"
And off rode Rastaman to his contented life

And so the story goes… of a Rastaman, him bicycle and him light
The judge it was said, later resigned
and went to live on the hills way up on high
And as for the policeman, he transferred to the day shift
in the Rosedale Heights.

Listen to the sound an' the beat of yu heart
Listen to the rebels an' the Rasta dem a talk
Listen to them chanting... listen to dem rapping
Listen to the shifting of the planet that is happening

With Criminal Intent

They wrapped their hatred around him
a hollow tip dum de dum dum dum
blow his black head to pieces
since he was just a blackity black black blackkk
wohoose tight minds into blackout
into thinking that everytime they see we
one of us
they have to account to a soul
brutality deception crunched into centuries
the horror the horror the horror

If we could just dance
and disappear
blunt instruments that plowed the fields
served the plantations
this house of capitalist plenty
that jack and every jack one a we build
no Jackman want to say it was built
by plunder, exploitation, murder, bondage and rape
making the Black print blue
and even losing that too

They carried their hatred, psychic scar
cocked on a trigger
set to blow away forever
a black boy's right to exist, to justice, to imperfection

On a dowdy Mississauga street in December '88
just after Christmas
and you know what Christmas is like
all that good cheer and so much greed
the Kangaroos struck
black blackity black black black blackkk
blackout

A cowardly aim
a decidedly, deliberate, privately purchased
banned, illegal bullet
and you don't have to join the ku klux klan anymore

They wrapped their hatred around him
heaped up bursting out
they had to let it off somewhere
and since you and you and you and you were out of sight
they hurled spite on this young son
and blow his blackity black black blakkk head to pieces
black blackity blackity blackity blackity blackkk
blackout

I tell you
justice is swift
with a fullness of criminal intent
at the end of an illegal bullet
when you face your serve-and-protectors
your jury, your executioner and judge

Unnatural Causes

WOOoooooooOOOoooooo

The wind howled and cussed
it knew no rest
when it ran free it was a hurricane
to be watched and silenced

silence makes you sit and rot
even cactus fades
against persistent drought

they hope the poor will become acclimatized
see how they look at skyrises
and call them mountain peaks
see how the sun greets them first
in the city
makes a rolling shadow

bong ... bong ... bong ... bong ... bong ...

Somewhere in this silvered city
hunger rails beneath the flesh
... and one by one, they're closing shops
in the city
... the Epicure, the Rivoli on the Porch ...

No small affair
... No small affair — the sequel ... Le Petit Café
the Bamboo ...

The city, a curtained metropolitan glare
grins a diamond sparkle sunset
It cuts a dashing pose

"The picture you sent on the postcard
was wonderful!
It reminded me of a fairyland
where everything is so clean
a place where everyone is happy
and well taken care of

... and the sky ... the sky ... it seems so round, so huge
and so indifferent"

Indifference passes through the wind
the wind, it rains a new breed
breeds a new passion
the passion of inaction
the inaction of politicians
the art of avoiding issues
the issues of culture
the culture of exclusion
the exclusion of the 'political'
and the powerless
bong ... bong ... bong ... bong ... bong ...

Somewhere in this our city
in our governing chambers
a watershed of indelight
of neutered niceties, unctuous
Click/ / /click/ / /click

postcard perfect

Dry rivers in the valley
the thirst at the banks of plenty
the room at the street-car shelter
a bus stop bed
   a bus stop bed
     a bus stop bed

You can make it through winter if you're ice
You can make it through winter if you're ice

gone frozen
on many things
bare back. no shelter
ice hearts in the elements
impassioned is the wind

All people are created equal except in winter
All people are created equal except in winter

Right here
on the front steps of abundance
Caroline Bungle tugs her load
stalks a place, invites a little company of sleep

unclick/ / /
this my dear is very unpostcardlike

Not inclined to poses
posturing only her plight
a dungle of terror
of lost hope
abandonment
an explorer in the arctic of our culture
a straggler adrift
cross our terrain of indifference
a life unravelled
seeks a connection
a soul outstretched to the cosmos

Can you spare a little social change, please?
a cup of tea
a place to sleep
a job
  a job
    a job …???

"The last postcard you sent was kinda weird
… poor people, sleeping at the bus stop!??
Surely you don't have that there …"

"… anyways, I'm dying to come to Canada
I'm a pioneer!"

In These Canadian Bones

In these Canadian bones
where Africa landed
and Jamaica bubble
inna reggae redstripe
and calypso proddings of culture
We are creating this very landscape
we walk on

My daughter sings opera
speaks perfect Canadian
And I dream in dialect
grown malleable by my Canadian tongue
of a world where all that matters is
the colour of love/compassion/heart
and music that grooves you

And I care about Québec
not just for Montréal
that pulsing city in heat
whose hips I want to stride
but for the tempo of language
stride and stridency in ownership of culture
not the hot air facism
distinct of Bouchard
but the way they love jazz

And I thank Indigenous peoples for this country
a guest on this planet
we all are, I tell you

Revolution from de Beat

Revolution from de drum
Revolution from de beat
Revolution from de heart
Revolution from de feet

De riddim and the heave and the sway of the beat
de rumblings and the tumblings down
to the dreams to the beat. To the impulse to be free
to the life that spring up in the heat   in the heat
in the pounding dance to be free
to bust open a window
crash upon a door
strip the crust of confinement
seep truth, through cracks
through the routing rhythms of the musical tracts   tracks

De sound of reggae music came on a wave of patter   patter
of deeply rooted internal chatter   chatter
on wings of riddim and melodies gone free
the bass strum the heart
the bass drum the heart beat
and the Rastaman pound! Bong bong   bong bong
beat them drums mon! Bong bong   bong bong

And de sound all around
and the voice
of impulse crafted into life burning darkness
of light
of days journeying through night

of riddim pulse wails and dreams
and determination to be free
of sight
of a vision that ignites
of a musical bam-bam fling-down-baps get-up-stand-up jam!
A musical realignment of the planets
a joy and a singing for those on it

Liberation impulse
dig the colonialists' grave

crunch of the sixties
baton carried through civil rights flames
spirit of the hippies
signify new ways
the Black power five
the right-on jive
women raise banners for their rights
communities organize
and workers struggle for human rights   for human rights

De core of the African self
separated by four hundred years
ties blighted and nipped   a continental divide
and colonialist lies
a sip from the being of the African well
uncorked the primal African self
and woo...oosh woo...oo...oosh the well spring up
and a riddim let loose
and reggae music found us

It was the pulse in the Caribbean that echoed bright
a voice on a beat
squashed determination released
and the wondrous sighs of Black people once again rose high
from a little piece of rock called Jamaica
where Arawak-speaking Tainos and Carib bones lie
came a breath of resistance
of peace love and liberation
spread worldwide on the wings of its artists and shaman
the bass and drums prance like a winded fire
chenke ckenke chenke chenke of a guitar strum
songs of freedom
of spirit
of love
of redemption

Revolution from de drum
Revolution from de beat
Revolution from de heart
Revolution with de feet
Ah   revolution

Rub A Dub Style Inna Regent Park

Monday morning broke
news of a robbery
Pam mind went
couldn't hold the load
dem took her to the station
a paddy wagon
screaming ...
her Johnny got a gun
from an ex-policeman

Oh Lawd, Oh Lawd Oh Lawd eh ya
a wey dis ya society a do
to wi sons

Rub a dub style
inna Regent Park
mon a dub it inna dance
inna Regent park
oh lawd oh lawd

"forget yu troubles and dance"
forget yu bills them
an irie up yuself
forget yu dreams of gathering dusts
on the shelves

dj rapper hear im chant
pumps a musical track
for im platform
cut it wild
sey de system vile
dubbing it inna dance
frustration pile
a different style
inna Regent Park

could have been a gun
but's a mike in his hand
could've been a gun spilling out the lines

but is a mike
  is a mike
    is a mike

Oh Lawd Oh Lawd Oh Lawd   eh ya

riddim line vessel im ache
from im heart outside
culture carry im past
an steady im mind
man tek a draw an feeling time
words cut harsh   try to find
explanations
de sufferings of de times

"forget yu troubles and dance"
forget yu bills dem
an irie up yu self
forget yu dreams gatherin

dust   dust   dust

is a long time wi sweating here
is a long time wi waiting here
to join society's rites
is a long time wi beating down yu door

is a long time since wi mek the trip
cross the Atlantic
on the slave shippppppp
is a long long time wi knocking
an every time yu slam the door
sey: no job
discrimination   injustice
a feel the whip lick
an is the same boat
  the same boat
    the same boat

Oh Lawd   Oh Lawd   Oh Lawd eh ya

dj chant out cutting it wild
sey one hav fi dub it inna different style

when doors close down on society's rites
windows will prey open
in the middle of the night
dashed hopes run wild
in the middle of the night
Oh Lawd   Oh   Lawd   Oh Lawd   eh ya

Dark Winds

Dark winds choked on the icy air
frustration was breathing
pleasure found ease
in the music beating pounding
bass line driving stroving
slap to the guitar hot licks
stirring up a musical commotion
the notion a rebel reggae rebel-motion

Man and woman and youth and I one
seeped in a voyage of discovery
a mystic deep black journey
the denseness and the blackness of the glory
glowing shining
the past and the present well aligning

What the people have to do nowadays mi say
if them work hard in a dance hall, ina house yard
ina school yard
just a uggle fi get a little space

and the haste and the waste
how them lay them bare
cause them black, cause them black
and the system justa progress pon them back
pon them back

and de music jus a beat
an the dance hall a rock
yu coulda hear
the feeling of gladness
mixed with hope jus a crackle
and the music jusa beat
in the heat of de sweat
and the tiredness and emptyness regress

Delroy and Imogene stood by the wall
cotch it up like if them move it woulda did drop
roll a crackle and a clap
a youth mouth burn;
"riddim! journey forward!"

and the p'lice them outside
couldn't stand the noise
that the heat and the beat and the mystic mists
was a blowing winds of glory
in a reggae creation story

and BAM!
them kick down the door
put everyone pon the floor
face down flat, face down flat

It was a brutal attack
pon the spirit of survival
pon the culture and the spirit of revival
pon de youth of Jane & Finch
cause them black, cause them black

what the people have to do today mi say
just a uggle fi get a little peace
and the haste and the waste
how them lay them bare
cause them black cause them black
and the system just a progress pon them back
pon them back

but our youths of today
just haffi find a way
fi stand them ground
and fight back
and fight back
and fight back

I Fight Back

ITT ALCAN KAISER
Canadian   Imperial Bank of Commerce
these are privilege names in my country
but I am illegal here

My children scream
My grandmother is dying

I came to Canada
found the doors of opportunity
well guarded

I scrub floors
serve backra's meals on time
spend two days working in one
twelve days in a week

Here I am in Canada
bringing up some else's child
while someone else and me in absentee
bring up my own

AND I FIGHT BACK

And constantly they ask
"Oh beautiful tropical beach
with coconut tree and rum
why did you leave there
why on earth did you come?"

AND I SAY:
For the same reasons
your mothers came

I FIGHT BACK

They label me
Immigrant, law-breaker, illegal, minimum wage worker
refugee
Ah no, not mother, not worker, not fighter

I FIGHT BACK
I FIGHT BACK
I FIGHT BACK

Feminism 101

Instead of being the doormat
get up and be the door

Good Womanhood (Censorship)

She builds her life
the latest TV shows
tailored emotions
rock 'n' roll radio

was the woman
a good woman should be
laboured at work
her boss' dream
laboured at home
no life
time of her own
lived through her man
only good women can

then the children came
and the smile and the charm
and the goodness of her heart
could no longer hold together
the shattering parts

twenty-five years
she balanced that life
knife-edge of good womanhood

then the civil rights movement came
opened up a door
Black peoples' and women's movements came
it opened up some more

she took a class
joined a club
got involved for the first time
on the picket lines

at the age of fifty-nine
climbed out of sublime

and that song of Bob Marley rattles in her head
'ah feel like bombing a church when I found out
the preacher was lying'

and she found out the TV was lying
and she found out the newspaper was lying
and she found out the government was lying
at the age of fifty-nine
a woman in her prime
like a river up a mountain
where the sun explodes
climbs out of sublime

and into the clearing

Billie Holiday

Oh Billie you lived on your drawl
sounds swirling out of black
rainbows splintering
through deceptions of greys
to your omniscient blues

so full of self
of music
in-your-face proud

passions burst into words
pride aches heartbeat
and slow defiance
note by note
Bessie's swing converges
Louis Armstong blowing language
breaking words apart
scat scat scattering soul
all over art   all over american culture

Billie's lips give shapes and hues to longings
meditation on deep spirit
on pain of being
elusive love
motions in the blood
fire and history from the bones
Billie's voice a poet's ease
and all that sass

To a Jazz Musician (Contemplating Suicide)

In the beginning was a lone jazz musician
played the first note
nucleus of the sun began to take
rippled off a few bars
layers of mountains came dancing
the tune got spicier
waterfalls broke through
slowed and got spacy
the atmosphere took its place
movement and timing
separated night and day
the music played and the song diffused
trees flowers rivers and seas took roots

In the beginning the Jazz musician played
didn't put that instrument down
until the seventh day

Jazz musician you are your notes and knows
and knows not
mind cannot comprehend limits of structure
time and space intrude
when rhythms of creation pulse through you
spiced by your impulse,
let's commit Jazz

Ja/Ja/Ja/Ja   Jazz

create a new universe
in here
out there
somewhere!

Ja/Ja/Ja/Ja   Jazz

The Poetry of Things

There is a place where no language goes
where fear is a door
where the mind comes to the edge of itself
reaches beyond
finds itself where heartbeats are born
in the deep black comfort of life's passages
nothing to declare or defend
where infinity struggles to measure itself
in the perfect world of imperfection
the place from which poetry springs

Everything well and wonderful is poetry

The idea that through the creative imagination we can reorder our world
and create a thing of enduring beauty is the essential idea of poetry

All that is visionless and full of despair is wounded poetry

Giving birth is the model for all new and revolutionary ideas
When we create a poem, we also give birth to new vibrations,
new rhythms, new ways of seeing, new ways of knowing
and new possibilities in the world.

The work of the poet is that of a midwife and birth mother

Poets materialize something into our world
that only exists before in sameness, or in fragments
or sometimes in ugliness and in pain.

Writing poetry is work of the soul.
Poetry is that dialogue between the world inside of us
and the world outside.

Possibilities for poetry arise when the heart reaches and puts
itself into words or brings itself into the existences of images.

Truth and beauty seek expression through the soul.

The act of writing is also the act of naming; of calling into being
Poetry brings into sharp focus the camera of one's mind's eye.

The poet sees with the soul.

The mind's eye sharpens and outlines. The soul reaches
to pull focus, to grasp the essence of things, to resonate with
that which vibrates most with beauty and truth.

Life is a way of being   Art is a way of seeing

The essence of life is its possibilities
Possibilities arise with vision.

Life is inherently challenged to express itself beyond   all possibilities
That is the poetry of life.

Everything well and wonderful is poetry

We bring the intensity of poetry to our lives
when we seek the essence of things – see possibilities
in everything around us. We can laugh more often, weep more
openly and seek to occupy the terrain of creativity and
imagination as a right.

In the territory of the creative imagination
we connect the in and outside
touch notion of life
creativity
the creator self
; wellspring of touch
sparks between two fingertips
closeness of touch
the perfect world of imperfection

Such is the poetry of life

Everything well and wonderful is poetry

PO   E   3

R   h   y   t   h   m

Riddim

rebel   revolt
resistance

R   e   vo   lu   t   i   on

if these words are not poetic
then poetry has no means to free me

One Poem Town

Hey!   Hey!   Hey!
this is a one poem town
this is a one poem town

ride in on your macrame verses
through barber-green minds
keep it kool! kool! kool!
on the page
'cause, if yu bring one in
any other way
we'll shoot you with metaphors
tie you cordless
hang you in ironies
drop a pun 'pon yu toe
and run you down, down, down
and out of town
'cause, this is a one poem town

and hey! what yu doing here anyway?

so don't come with no pling, ying, jing
ding something
calling it poetry
'cause, this is a one poem town
and you're not here to stay

Are you?

Riddim An' Hardtimes

An' him chucks on some riddim
    an' yu hear him say
        riddim an' hardtimes
          riddim an' hardtimes

music a prance
dance inna head
drumbeat a roll
hot like lead

Mojah Rasta gone dread
natt up natt up
irie
red

riddim a pounce wid a purpose
Truths and Rights
mek mi hear yu

drum
drum drum
drumbeat
heart beat
pulse beat
drum

roots wid a Reggae resistance
riddim
noh Dub them call it
riddim an' hardtimes

dem pound out the music
carv out the sounds
hard hard
hard like lead
an it bus im in im belly
an' a Albert Johnson
Albert Johsnon dead
dead
dead

but this ya country hard eh?
ah wey wi come ya fa?
wi come ya fi better
dread times
Jah signs

drum beat
pulse beat
heart beat
riddim an' hardtimes
riddim an' hardtimes
riddim an' hard
           hard
           hard

Liberation   Comes

liberation comes slowly
sometimes
a burglar in your sleep
        a crack
             doubt
                     an affirmation

peek on possibilities
and answers will come   barefoot

                     and
naked
prop on your doorstep
          and beat at your door

if you open to peek

it rushes in
like a flood

down a laneway

can't just ignore it like a beggar
when you go by

I Dream a Redwood

Last night I dream I was a Redwood
on the mountain side
a thousand three-hundred years old
breathe out pure oxygen
working morning and night
for this beautiful planet
all for life

I dream people love and admire me
say how wondrous this world
trees, animals, persons and things
can all breathe

I wish you were a Redwood
how great we would understand
the love and care it takes
to appreciate this land

I dream you were beside me
standing tall and growing strong
the earth we share
flesh dirt and spirit
our blood, our bond

Oh oh to be a wise old Redwood
a great big heart of wood
oh oh to be a Redwood

dreaming
dreaming tales

Liberation

You speak as if my liberation
is a one-way fare
you act as if my liberation
is some ill retreat
with naked bodies
and wooden dolls
try to take your hand from your blinded eyes

You say I should not try to undo
the image you hold of me
does it shake your world when I start to undo
your image of what I should do
the aged myths in which you've hidden me
it's time to take your hands from your blinded eyes

My friend, my liberation
didn't come from imagining
my friend, my liberation
didn't come from chasing dreams
there was hunger silence sweat
it's time to take your hands from your blinded eyes

All I am declaring
is that I have the same right
to be myself as you do
colour my own image as you do
yes I have the same right

to live for myself as you do
to find my way as you do
to make mistakes as you do
yes I have the same right

A Poem Against Things

There is no other time or place
to sing   tear up a book
or write a poem

Land so strange a dream
work day after day
another constructed smile
another wretched penny saved

I write poems
like a weapon
oh why oh why
and when will it end

Thursdays I meet
planning protest
slavery's ghost rise up
fury in their heads

War dance on Ottawa, Washington
brothers and sisters wrestle
South Africa to the ground
bury apartheid dead

Morning pulls the dawn
from deep South African nights
Azania strong and free

There is no other time or place
to sing
tear up a book
or write a poem
but here and now

Pandemic

One.
The year 2020 time reversed
the world into a pause
to search the lost and found
for meaning
misplaced things

Frantic we grope in quarantine
Within (our)selves
But not quarantined from our fears
and a conscience grown thin

How can we fathom that stepping out your door
Or going to the supermarket
to get groceries
or to meet up with friends at dusk
could be a death sentence?

Ask any young Black man.

Two.
In social isolation we rest
Become restless, the unknown looming
Weighty words;
lockdown, shelter-in-place,
social-distance, self-isolation,
quarantine
infection-count, intubate
Death-toll

Words screaming for submission

Three.
There is an enormity to the immensity
of this pandemic moment
A glum impenetrable disquietude
The anthropocene like worms in cottonwood

Four.
We've been moving
through life like it's our first feast

paid by an anonymous benefactor
with infinite generosity

Eyes aglitter, everywhere

Five.
People say it's a sign
Greed of the world's ruling classes has gone too far

we have given up too much of our personal values;

Flittering

Our Flitter an accomplice
to the pain of the othered

Six.
Now woke-ing from a universal drowning
in busy and significance   with our Things
We flitter; where to put our efforts
like where to put your eyes in feelings of shame

Seven.
Then the George Floyd murder
Twisted our necks
And we couldn't look away
Our Flitter weighted
As we held our breath
Didn't breathe   until

In a collective gasp
we found
A voice
to exhale

Eight.
The streets became our canvas
and the silence of the internet clicked and clonked
till community emerged
coalesced around the horror of racism we all know,
gas-lighted for decades

Nine.
Black people are harmed by the spit and the spite
Of white people turning away
Even above systemic inequalities and white supremacy
Pressing on our necks

Ten.
The year 2020 the world changed
before white folks did
before white folks did enough
before white folks did enough to courage-up
to fight against anti-Black racism

Eleven.
We are all in this together

Twelve.
Are we all in this together?

Thirteen.
Embrace this poem

Fourteen.
Talk back to this poem with your heart, gentle

Revolutionary Tea Party

You who know what the past has been
you who work in the present tense
you who see through to the future
come mek wi work together

come sit here with we
a mek wi drink tea
a mek wi talk
a mek wi analyse

You who have been burned by vanguardism
come mek wi give yu little nurturing
come sit awhile
a mek wi drink tea
a mek wi talk
a mek wi strategize

You who believe in the future
in transforming by your labour
let the future be in good favour

We who create the wealth of the world
only get scrapings from them in control
when wi siddown and look at the system
check out the way that things been
wi haffi say ... wi haffi say
the system in a really bad way

A wey it a defend?

You who see for peace a future
you who understands the past
you who create with yu sweat from yu heart
let's talk, let's make art, let's love, dance
revel in the streets if that's the beat
protest demonstrate chant

You who see us for a future
come sit here with we
mek wi drink tea

mek wi talk
mek wi analyse
mek wi strategize
mek wi work together

Dis Word

dis word breeds my rhythm
dis word carries my freedom
dis word is my hand
:   my weapon

Afterword
Tuning the Heart with Poetry

I don't think of four white walls, silence, and solitude when I think of how to understand or engage with my poetry. I think of community. I think of clapping and a stomping of feet, of resisting instead of giving up.

My words listen for the pause, the weeping and soaring in the hearts of readers and listeners—of those who long for a better, more equitable world.

Works in *Make the World New* were written over several decades. Only one poem, "Pandemic," was created for this collection. In it, I had to mark the confluence of two major historic and transformative moments in our time. One is the pandemic of 2020 wrought by nature with consequences of grave enormity. The other is Black Lives Matter, a protracted movement gaining worldwide momentum with its demands against state and police brutality, specifically the murders of Black people. That convergence allowed for and supercharged the fight against anti-Black racism and demands for equal rights and justice for all.

> *How can we fathom stepping out your door*
> *Or going to the supermarket*
> *To get groceries*
> *Or meet up with friends at dusks*
> *Could be a death sentence?*
>
> *Ask any young Black man*

I love being a poet, and that's being a writer also. I love being called a poet. I often smile and ask myself: how did this happen? It feels like I have gotten away with something extraordinary. It sure feels good.

The Universe and poetry are interchangeable concepts for me. As a poet my journey is to figure out what I can know for self and others, to discern what can be understood and to spar with what is real and what is not. This journey tangles with the proverbial human project grounded on a rock we call earth, which holds an abundance of water and brims with species. A tango with a patient, faithful, and weighted moon that glides relentlessly in a circle through space, preening for a glowing ball of fire, perhaps waiting for a supernova.

Would it be unreasonable to propose that how we attempt to understand in the granular and untangle these relationships for ourselves is the substance of poetry?

Growing up in Jamaica, children were made to revere and fear books. Authors, mostly male, occupied what seemed to be an impenetrable world giving us things of such import that the thoughts and motivations behind the lines on the page had to be studied, dissected and speculated on.

Their words moved and stirred us, making us see/understand a particular version of reality, their version, which we were called to believe was a "universal" one. Poetry was lofty business it seemed. The Jamaican poet Louise Bennett's poetry and performance captured my imagination and resonated in my bones, yet she (at that time) was not held in the esteem of the poets we were made to study and honour. I felt called to writing and sharing my work but I did not dream that one day I would join the ranks of poets who would be read, appreciated, and studied.

For some this would not be a big deal. For me it was something that felt unattainable. I knew how I could become a doctor, a lawyer or even prime minister. So imagine my glee, my delight, to fall into the writing life. To land beautifully in resonance and relevance.

Papers and thesis on my work cause me to marvel at how academics, critics and grassroots readers and listeners engage with the consciousness of my poems illuminating the possibilities of the lines—sometimes making me sound really very smart. It makes me smile.

I love being a poet!

I love being a poet. As that artist, I save stories and find ideas that can ease hearts, heal some pain and provoke the imaginary. I'm sure it's the way a doctor feels when they heal flesh and body, when they save lives.

My Poetry allows me to turn fixed notions of race, gender, grassroots aspirations and social relations upside-down and sideways. It brings various parts of community, self, knowing, experience, knowledges, and contexts to front and centre, and can help to counter the fragmentation, marginalization, and demoralization that contemporary life demands. It can connect disparate souls.

A collection of poems in a book like this can become an object—but for the spoken word artist or dub poet, language is alive, and these poems should always be alive in community. Aliveness in our work is an important way to intervene with realities that cement prescribed ways of being in our hierarchies of social arrangements.

If we are all stories, we are different stories to different people in different segments of our stratified society. Stepping outside of the colonizing white gaze, writers like Toni Morrison explore who Black people are for ourselves. The body of her work demonstrates than when our story is written by others, we cannot be the centre, the very heartbeat of our own stories.

The poet sees patterns in everything and can roll backward and forward, on rhythms from the past into the future. Rhythm is spatial, it is vibratory. It spaces patterns by beats, whether it's the beat of a century, or the beat of a moment, or the beats in the lines of the poem. They guide us to discover what's inscribed in poems, the torque between the lines, the hole between the spaces.

The idea of knowing and making meaning is less an aesthetic practice and more about positioning ourselves/us in a world where others are looking on from fixed positions and practices.

We are narratives, we exist in the storied nature of things: "Yu born/ yu live/and then yu die." Even fragmentary non-narrative elucidations so important to poetry are parts of the story, and every story is a narrative and aesthetic pattern that helps us to make sense of things.

Another of poetry's big jobs is to distinguish specificity,

illuminate musk in the darkness;
see the singer and the song
bring aspects of silence alive
grasp for truth in a sea of science and nature
enrich cultural, spiritual and universal imaginaries
Seeking, searching, wanting, questioning
; and that pause "to let the world in"
Poetry's a singular gesture, a belief
that revitalizes language

Poetry connects language and eye by drawing our attention to detail and to vivid, concrete and contemplative ideation. Poetry's metaphor invents, holds breath, breathes out, and pulls from the art of dance to create its work of art. Crayons, scissors, two new pair of glasses, one turned inward and one turned outward, some fine sandpaper instead of duct tape, rhythm and sound weave words, images, emotions together.

> *Meaning.*
> *Meaning can be*
> *Meaning is*
> *Meaning's deductibility.*

A couple of years ago, I landed at Heathrow airport for a thirteen-stop, UK-to-Paris reading/performance and lecture tour. The immigration officer looked at my "bank account" outfit and was very pleased. I always dress in recognizably expensive clothes when I travel to "first world" countries. It seems to mitigate the "random"/not so random selection that always singles me out for further questioning at these crossings. I do the opposite for my travel to third world countries. In every passport there is a code that tells the immigration officer your professional designation. So when they ask what you do, as this officer did, it is really a trick question. To his question, I said, "I'm a writer, a poet." That seemed to have given him pause: "Well, what else? He was encouraging me with his hands giving me a hint. "Do you mean Professor?" I said. He seemed relieved by the "correct" answer. Then he asked sing-songy and all: "Which do you like better?" "Oh, I love being a poet," I told him. His face lit up. He smiled, leaned in and whispered as if to share a secret: "I write poetry too." No more questioning. He stamped my passport. "Welcome to the UK," he said, and waved me on, still smiling.

I love being a poet.

In another border crossing and poetic encounter, the US immigration officer was a Black woman. Old tags on my travel bags and the variety of stamps in my passport triggered an alarm in her colleague and I heard the phrase "frequent traveler." Two additional immigration officers and a dog descended on my travel bags prodding, squeezing and sniffing. "I'm just a poet," I said. One of the officers heard the word "prophet" instead and seemed alarmed.

Whatever it was the authorities thought they might find in my bags, they didn't, and were quickly called to another more "suspicious" traveler.

"You're a poet, eh?" said the Black woman immigration officer as she returned her focus to me.

"Yep," I said, "I love being a poet!"

She held up my book *Women Do This Every Day*, and thumbed through, tilting her head as if to see it from different angles. She tarried. She seemed to read a few lines here and there and nodded her head approvingly. When she looked at me again, she said "if you're a real poet, recite me a poem." I did (and gladly). In those three minutes between words we existed in a different universe. When I finished, she shouted down the line: "We got a poet here, we got a poet here! We got a real poet here!" She had a joyous look on her face as she waved me through and was still waving when I looked back. I smiled all the way on the long flight to Seattle.

I love, love, love being a poet!

When I first started writing, I understood little about the formalities and technicalities of poetry. I understood metaphor simply as a way of powerfully cementing meaningful connections by making it so in language. I understood that although a poet starts out writing about the thing or idea, the poem itself becomes a thing in a different family of "knowing." What I admire about poetry is how we are made to tarry in kernels of language, the evocative nature of poetics and beyond the page to experience gestures, sounds and acoustic effects, to find new meanings and insights and how we are brought to pause from the world in order to focus on the world. I delight in the way a cluster of words, a phrase turned "jus soh" can open the imagination and spark all sorts of connections and things. I think of that space in my poetry as political, where I reach out as poet, and the reader/listener reaches inside themselves to connect to my words.

Poetic language is an instigator for new spaces, for the breath and freedoms in its attempt at beauty.

My Poems are questions or assertions that challenge the status quo and are seen as provocative. I prefer to know them as subversives.

I assert that poetry doesn't have to be about lofty, obscure, academic or highfalutin things. Poetry must also belong to the people and it is effective when it reflects, validates, and celebrates the rigors of the everyday which are important to most of the world's population.

Poetry is a breath that flows through my bones and my skin and a mother-tongue that is not my own or my mother's. Through the din of hegemonic culture, I hear the ancestors and the echo from the constant future. Somewhere in the unknowable, I feel open possibilities.

The cultural coded sound of the voice
and vernacular
is a source of pleasure, shared
Decentering listening with the sharable,
new meanings and new imperatives
in order to be accountable.

On my tongue the language I know carves its way
slow dances, wears away at its own (claustro)phobias
auto-conscious colonizing tendencies.
Language vibrates in my ear as invention
sends the imagination skipping stones.

In 2020, the world changed before most people did.

Jamaican dub poet Mutabaraka says poetry is the poet's weapon "blazin for freedom" (1986). Writing for me has always been a liberatory assertion, an aesthetic practice of freedom and resistance, and, as Lisa Tomlinson writes, dub poetry is "a literary art of decolonization" (2017, 59).

I ask you, what do my poems make present for you? What emotions do they stir up in you? What are they trying to get you to see and understand? Do my poems continue to work after they have been read or listened to? Are my poems activist? Subversive?

Read these poems so you can hear the roll and curvature of the language. Let the poems take you inside the words, around the words, beyond the words, and beyond the page—their rhythmic beats and stresses re-orienting you. Find patter and patterns in these poems. Look for the emotional subtext in each line, in each poem. For the student, you may also want to ask what devices, literary and non-literary, are deployed in each poem to contribute to the message, effects, and achievement of the work. Speculate on the claims these poems make separately and together.

I want for readers to enjoy the art of my expression and to be with the ideas this collection has placed before you. These poems ask you to "read" beyond the page, to move beyond the words laying still on the page, to bring your heart into the picture and to talk back fearlessly (but gently) to these poems.

—*Lillian Allen*

Works Cited

Mutabaruka. "Dis Poem." *The Mystery Unfolds*, LP. Newton, NJ: Shanachie Records, 1986.

Tomlinson, Lisa. *The African-Jamaican Aesthetic: Cultural Retention and Transformation Across Borders*. Leiden and Boston: Brill/Rodipi, 2017.

Acknowledgements

To the spirit of Thelma Allen (mi modha), who went on to complete three university degrees after the age of sixty.

And mi sista Olive Allen Morris-Whitehead

I dedicate this collection to little Phia, my granddaughter.

To her amazing mom; dis little girl mi call Anta.

To my god/soul son Sam.

To the nephews and nieces all over the place.

To all my art sons and daughters – you know who you are.

To my many inspiring students – thanks for letting me be your teacha.

To the Toronto reggae community who provide a psychic grounding and sites of connectivity for Jamaican people and culture in this metropole of the north.

And to Spanish Town, St. Jago de la Vega, old time 'Panish Town people dem, their ancestors and descendants – big up oonu self!

—*Lillian Allen*

To Lillian, thanks for the words, the revolution and di riddim.

Respect to Michael Bucknor, my teacher, who first introduced me to the poetry of Lillian Allen.

Phanuel Antwi, Faizal Deen, Kaie Kellough, Nalini Mohabir, I love being in intellectual and poetry community with you in this place called Canada. Iron sharpening iron.

Finally, my unending thanks and love to my mother who has taught me so many things about the word and the world.

—*Ronald Cummings*

"Queenie Queenie and the Fall of Colonial Empire" was first published as a short story in *Lish: A Journal in the Foreigner's English* Vol 1, December 2020. "Trust" appeared in *cmagazine 139*, Autumn 2018. Both these works have been revised for publication here.

"Broken" was published as a poem of the week at *Split This Rock* on June 28, 2013. http://blogthisrock.blogspot.com/2013/06/

"JAMAICA - I Remember" was published in *Jubilation!: Poems Celebrating 50 years of Jamaican Independence* edited by Kwame Dawes (Leeds: Peepal Tree Press, 2012) and also appeared on *Anxiety* (Toronto: Verse to Vinyl, 2012).

"The Wait of History," "The Poetry of Things," "Song for Newfoundland," "Rasta in Court," "Billie Holiday," "In these Canadian Bones," and "Revolution from de Beat" were published in *Psychic Unrest* (Toronto: Insomniac Press, 1999). The version of "The Poetry of Things" that appears in this volume has been revised.

"Nellie Belly Swelly," "My Momma," "Birth," "To The Child," "Conditions Critical," "Nicaragua," "Dictator (For Haiti)," "Could it Happen in America," "With Criminal Intent," "Unnatural Causes," "Rub A Dub Style Inna Regent Park," "Dark Winds," "Feminism 101," "Good Womanhood (Censorship)," "To a Jazz Musician (Contemplating Suicide)," "PO E 3," "One Poem Town," "Liberation Comes," "I Dream a Redwood," "Revolutionary Tea Party," and "Dis Word" were published in *Women Do This Every Day* (Toronto: Women's Press, 1993). The versions of "Birth" and "Could It Happen in America" which appear in this volume have been revised.

"Marriage," "Liberation," "Riddim an' Hardtimes," "I Fight Back," and "A Poem Against Things" were published in *Rhythm an' Hardtimes* (Toronto: Domestic Bliss Publishers/Flash Frontline Publications, 1982). The version of "Marriage" that appears in this volume has been revised.

lps Books in the Laurier Poetry Series
Published by *Wilfrid Laurier University Press*

Kateri Akiwenzie-Damm
(Re)Generation: The Poetry of Kateri Akiwenzie-Damm, selected with an introduction by Dallas Hunt, with an afterword by Kateri Akiwenzie-Damm • 2021 • xx + 74 pp. • ISBN 978-1-77112-471-3.

Lillian Allen
Make the World New: The Poetry of Lillian Allen, edited by Ronald Cummings, with an afterword by Lillian Allen • 2021 • xxii + 82 pp. • ISBN 978-1-77112-495-9

Nelson Ball
Certain Details: The Poetry of Nelson Ball, selected with an introduction by Stuart Ross, with an afterword by Nelson Ball • 2016 • xxiv + 86 pp. • ISBN 978-1-77112-246-7

derek beaulieu
Please, No More Poetry: The Poetry of derek beaulieu, edited by Kit Dobson, with an afterword by Lori Emerson • 2013 • xvi + 74 pp. • ISBN 978-1-55458-829-9

Dionne Brand
Fierce Departures: The Poetry of Dionne Brand, edited by Leslie C. Sanders, with an afterword by Dionne Brand • 2009 • xvi + 44 pp. • ISBN 978-1-55458-038-5

Di Brandt
Speaking of Power: The Poetry of Di Brandt, edited by Tanis MacDonald, with an afterword by Di Brandt • 2006 • xvi + 56 pp. • ISBN 978-0-88920-506-2

Nicole Brossard
Mobility of Light: The Poetry of Nicole Brossard, edited by Louise H. Forsyth, with an afterword by Nicole Brossard • 2009 • xxvi + 118 pp. • ISBN 978-1-55458-047-7

Alice Burdick
Deportment: The Poetry of Alice Burdick, edited by Alessandro Porco • 2018 • xxx + 64 pp. • ISBN 978-1-77112-380-8

Margaret Christakos
Space Between Her Lips: The Poetry of Margaret Christakos, edited by Gregory Betts, with an afterword by Margaret Christakos • 2017 • xxviii + 68 pp. • ISBN 978-1-77112-297-9

George Elliott Clarke
Blues and Bliss: The Poetry of George Elliott Clarke, edited by Jon Paul Fiorentino, with an afterword by George Elliott Clarke • 2008 • xviii + 72 pp. • ISBN 978-1-55458-060-6

Dennis Cooley
By Word of Mouth: The Poetry of Dennis Cooley, edited by Nicole Markotić, with an afterword by Dennis Cooley • 2007 • xxii + 62 pp. • ISBN 978-1-55458-007-1

Lorna Crozier
Before the First Word: The Poetry of Lorna Crozier, edited by Catherine Hunter, with an afterword by Lorna Crozier • 2005 • xviii + 62 pp. • ISBN 978-0-88920-489-8